# FONDUES

## MADE EASY

**ABIGAIL BROWN AND
MELISSA WEBB**

NEW HOLLAND

First published in the UK in 2005 by
New Holland Publishers (UK) Ltd
London Cape Town Sydney Auckland

Garfield House, 86–88 Edgware Road
London W2 2EA
United Kingdom
www.newhollandpublishers.com

80 McKenzie Street
Cape Town 8001
South Africa

Level 1, Unit 4, 14 Aquatic Drive
Frenchs Forest, NSW 2086
Australia

218 Lake Road
Northcote, Auckland
New Zealand

ISBN  1 84537 044 9

Senior Editor: Steffanie Brown
Production: Hazel Kirkman
Design: Roger Hammond@BlueGum
Photographer: Stuart West
Editorial Direction: Rosemary Wilkinson

Based on a design idea by Michele Gomes

1 3 5 7 9 10 8 6 4 2

Reproduction by Colourscan, Singapore
Printed and bound by Times Offset (M) Sdn Bhd, Malaysia

DEDICATION

MELISSA

To cheeky chappie Flynn – you rock.

ABI

To Big Bad Jas – you are my rock.

ACKNOWLEDGEMENTS

We would like to thank Steffanie Brown, our mad Canadian editor, for her support, but most of all for her sense of humour and crazy ways. We would also like to thank Stuart West, our photographer, for making us and our food look beautiful (hopefully!), and for entertaining us with all our favourite '80s hits. And of course we would like to thank each other: Thank you Abi, and thank you Mel! What a giggle we have had. Thanks also to our parents for their swinging '60s fondue stories, and to our friends for their input and ideas.

# FONDUES

## MADE EASY

## CONTENTS

# INTRODUCTION

Are you having friends over for a meal but can't think what to give them? How about a fondue? If you look in your mother's or grandmother's attic or at the back of a kitchen cupboard you are almost guaranteed to find a fondue set hiding from the 1960s! Just as popular then as it is today, fondue is a great way to get your friends or family together for a fun and informal lunch or dinner. The word *fondue* is derived from the French word "fondre", meaning "to melt" or "to blend". When most people think of fondue they think of snow-capped mountains in Switzerland, and of sitting around in a cozy chalet drinking kirsch and dipping bread into a bubbling pot of melted cheese. This is probably because fondue is originally the national dish of Switzerland. The traditional Swiss fondue, known as "Neuchâtel", is named after its canton of origin, and uses Gruyère and Emmenthal cheese (see page 17 for the recipe).

As much as we love the traditional cheese fondues, in this book we overstep traditional boundaries and show you that there are many other ways of using your fondue pot. In these pages you will find a wide variety of delicious fondue recipes – from hot garlic oil and simmering, flavourful stock fondues to rich, creamy chocolate and sticky marshmallow fondues. The wide range of "dippers" in our recipes are equally exciting and diverse, ranging from deliciously marinated meats to tangy dried fruits and mouthwatering vanilla cakes. Many of the recipes include a sauce to be dipped into after the food has been cooked in the fondue, for that extra bit of flavour. Our recipes are simple and quick to prepare and, hopefully, will give you the confidence to use your own creative flair to give life to your own fondue ideas!

As you will see from this book, serving fondue can be a relaxing way to host a party: your guests get to cook their own food, and you get to enjoy a leisurely evening socializing with your friends and family. As host, there is little for you to do after you have made your initial preparations: the raw ingredients are set out on the table, so all you need do is to join your guests in dipping the wonderful morsels of food presented! All kinds of dippers and dipping sauces can be prepared in advance, giving you more time with your guests – and less time in the kitchen. And because fondue makes for a longer, slower meal, you'll have plenty of time to chat with your guests and catch up on their news and gossip. We have both had some hilarious evenings together with our friends over a fondue and a couple of bottles of wine, and hope you will too. Happy dipping!

# EQUIPMENT

There are all kinds of fondue sets available from local shops these days. The most popular are earthenware, pottery, cast iron or metal and porcelain. It is important to use the right pot for your chosen fondue.

**EARTHENWARE OR POTTERY** Cheese fondue is traditionally made in earthenware or pottery pots, which resemble the original Swiss fondue pot, called a "caquelon". The pot is heated from underneath by a methylated spirit burner, or by using solid fuel, which is designed to fit into the burner. The pot is then placed on a stand, so that the bottom sits directly over the flame. Earthenware and pottery fondue pots are very heavy and thick, and there is a slow transmission of heat, which helps to stop the cheese from catching on the bottom of the pot. These pots are usually wider and more shallow than the other kinds of fondue pots, allowing you to swirl your bread in the melted cheese and cover it well. Earthenware and pottery pots should not be used for hot oil fondues, however, as they are shallow enough to be dangerous, and they don't get hot enough to heat the oil sufficiently. Take care when cleaning this type of fondue pot. If there is cheese stuck to it, let it soak in hot, soapy water before you attempt to clean it. Do not use any kind of abrasive cleaner, or you will scratch the surface of the pot, making the cheese stick even more the next time you use it.

**ENAMELLED CAST IRON OR STAINLESS STEEL** Cast iron or stainless steel fondue pots are typically used for hot oil or stock fondues, in which meat, poultry, fish or vegetables are cooked. These pots retain heat very effectively, keeping the liquid hotter for longer. They often come with a cover with fork rests in it, to keep the fondue forks still and prevent them from getting tangled up! These pots can also be used for cheese and chocolate fondues, as long as the heat is kept low.

**PORCELAIN** Porcelain pots are best for dessert fondues, such as chocolate or cream. They are generally smaller in size than the other types of fondue pots, and are heated gently by a small candle flame placed underneath the pot.

**SAFETY**
When giving a fondue party, never forget that you have a naked flame on the table. Make sure all your guests can reach the fondue pot with ease, so that they are not stretching too far. If female guests have trailing sleeves, it is advisable to roll them up (we have seen one guest's sleeve go up in flames!). Everyone should have enough space for their dipping bowls, plates and glasses. Avoid long-stemmed wine glasses that are easily knocked over.

Take special care when a hot oil fondue is being served, as nasty burns occur from a single drop of oil. Place your fondue pot stand on a stabilizing mat that will not let the pot slip. If, however, the pot does get knocked over and catches fire, DO NOT throw water on to it. Dampen a cloth and cover the flames with the cloth – this should stop the fire. Remember that fondue pots can get very hot, so always use an oven glove or a thick tea towel to pick one up.

If children are sharing the fondue, it is a good idea to give them their own individual plate of dippers, and to set a bowl of the fondue next to them to avoid them stretching across the table, which could be a recipe for disaster.

**INTERCHANGEABLE FONDUE POT** If you want to buy only one fondue pot for different dishes, you can buy an interchangeable fondue pot. These pots are usually made of stainless steel or copper, and come with a removable porcelain insert. They can be used for cooking a wide range of fondues, from stock and oil to cheese and chocolate.

**FORKS AND SKEWERS** You will usually find that fondue sets are sold in boxes containing the fondue pot, stand, burner and fondue forks. The forks are usually two pronged, and are mostly colour-coded or numbered so your guests know which fork is theirs! Bamboo skewers can also be used to spear food, and Chinese wire strainers are very useful for catching small pieces of vegetable in stock fondues, or for picking up dumplings.

**DIPPING BOWLS** If you are having a fondue party, add interest to your table with different dipping bowls and plates. They are so many beautiful plates and bowls available these days that there is no excuse for boring white china! If you are cooking with hot oil or serving breaded food, line the plates or bowls with absorbent paper for a tidier meal.

**KITCHEN KNIVES** Sharp kitchen knives are a must when preparing fondues featuring vegetables and meat. You don't need a huge range – we have used just three kinds of knife to prepare our recipes: a small vegetable knife with a smooth blade, a large (20-cm/8-in) knife for cutting meat, and a bread knife. Keep your knives separate from each other, storing them in a knife block if possible, to prevent them from getting blunt. Never put your knives in the sink, especially if it is full of water, and keep them sharp using a knife sharpener or steel.

**PEELER** This is a very useful tool for peeling both vegetables and fruits. It's also handy for shaving zest off lemons, limes and oranges.

**CHOPPING BOARD** Plastic chopping boards are being used more and more frequently these days. They are easy to keep clean, and do not retain the smell of garlic or onion in the way wooden boards do. Remember to clean your chopping board often, especially if you are preparing different kinds of foods. You don't want your chocolate fondue to taste of garlic or onions!

# INGREDIENTS

## BUYING AND STORING

If you are a lover of fondue, it is a good idea to keep a few basic ingredients in your cupboards so you can make one whenever the mood takes you. You don't have to buy everything that we have listed opposite, but these ingredients are useful for all kinds of cooking, as well as for fondue!

As with all cooking, the better the quality of the ingredients, the better the end product. So try to buy the best quality you can afford. When buying vegetables, make sure they are as fresh as possible, as you may not use them for a couple of days. When eating vegetables that have been lightly cooked in fondue, you want them to taste very fresh. Of course, if you can afford it, organic is the way to go for all foods, especially for vegetables. All kitchens should have such basic ingredients to hand as garlic, good-quality olive oil, sea salt, freshly ground black pepper and stock cubes – or, even better, home-made stock in the freezer.

In this book we use all kinds of different foods from various countries. Visit different supermarkets for a wider variety of foods, and look for local ethnic supermarkets near you that you may not have visited before. Seeing new ingredients will inspire new and creative ideas for your dinner or lunch parties. When it comes to buying meat and fish, a visit to your local butcher or fishmonger may be more lucrative than a visit to a supermarket, as these specialists can prepare meat and fish so it is ready to use. Be careful not to buy too many fresh ingredients, however, as many foods can go off quite quickly.

When you come home from food shopping, quickly put your ingredients into the refrigerator or freezer, as necessary. Ensure that open packs of food are always resealed or closed properly. When storing cheese, make sure that it is kept in an airtight container, or tightly wrapped with clingfilm (plastic wrap), to prevent it from going hard.

## KITCHEN CUPBOARD

Stock cubes: chicken, fish,
   beef, lamb

Olive oil

Sea salt

Black peppercorns

Honey

White wine vinegar

Pine nuts

Paprika

Cumin seeds

Peanut oil

Sesame oil

Vegetable oil

Peanut butter

Flour

Marshmallows

Chocolate: dark, plain, milk

Chocolate biscuits (cookies)

Wine: red and white

Dried fruits

Mango chutney

## KITCHEN SHELF

Fresh garlic

Fresh basil plant

Fresh bay leaves

Fresh parsley plant

Fresh coriander (cilantro)

## FRIDGE

Variety of cheeses

Butter

Grainy mustard

Dijon mustard

Selection of vegetables
   suitable for dipping:
   mangetout (snow peas),
   baby corn, red pepper, etc.

Bacon

Soft fruits

Cream

Fresh stuffed pasta

Tomato purée

Lemon juice

## FREEZER

Selection of breads that can
   be defrosted and used for
   dipping

Prawns

Kaffir lime leaves

Fresh root ginger (keeps well
   in the freezer)

Home-made frozen stock

Dumpling pastries

# PRESENTATION AND COOKING

When you are giving a party, presentation is obviously very important. Your guests will remember their evening all the more if each of their senses – sight, smell, hearing, touch and taste – are stimulated. Luckily, half the fun of entertaining is getting everything ready before your guests arrive. Decorating the table for a fondue party can be a creative experience, especially if there is a theme to your fondue night. For example, if you have chosen a Thai theme, you could cover your table with a banana leaf, use bamboo placemats, and serve the food in lined straw baskets. If you are making an Asian-inspired stock fondue, encourage your guests to use china spoons to drink the stock after the cooking is finished. If you decide on a Moroccan theme, perhaps decorate the room with Moroccan tea glasses with tea lights inside, and burn some cinnamon incense to get everyone in the mood! Whatever your chosen theme, if any, there is a huge range of beautiful dipping bowls and serving platters available these days, so let your imagination go wild.

When giving a fondue party, there are a few basic preparations you can make to help the evening run more smoothly. Giving each guest a different-coloured bowl will help them remember which bowl is theirs. If you have more than six guests, it is a good idea to have more than one fondue pot. Otherwise, your guests may have to wait inordinately long for a turn to dip into the pot! A round table is ideal for a fondue party, but don't worry if you don't have one – just make sure that all of your guests can easily reach the fondue pot and all the accompaniments on the table. Finally, we would avoid using long-stemmed glasses at a fondue party. As your guests stretch across the table to dip into the fondue pot, their glasses could easily get knocked over. We suggest using low wine glasses or coloured tumblers for this reason.

There are a few simple rules to follow in order to maintain the right temperature and consistency for your fondue for the duration of the evening. When cooking a cheese fondue, turn the heat down once the fondue is hot, and let the fondue gently bubble away slowly. Do not turn the heat off, or else the fondue will get cold and congeal. Also, keeping the heat on will allow the delicious "crouton" (a layer of slightly browned cheese) to form at the bottom of the pot. If your cheese fondue gets too thick, try adding a little more liquid, such as white wine or milk. When cooking in oil fondue, keeping the flame at a medium height will keep the oil at a high enough temperature to cook the food item properly. If the oil starts to smoke, however, be sure to turn the heat down! For a stock fondue, turn the heat down once it has come to the boil and keep it simmering gently. If the heat is too high, the fondue will evaporate away.

# CHEESE FONDUES

## CLASSIC NEUCHATEL FONDUE

serves 6

**INGREDIENTS**

1 clove garlic, cut in half

450 ml (16 fl oz/2 cups) dry white
   wine (Neuchâtel, Rhine or Chablis)

125 g (4 oz/1 cup) Emmenthal, cut
   into cubes

125 g (4 oz/1 cup) Gruyère, cut into
   cubes

3 tbsp cornflour

3 tbsp kirsch or brandy

salt

freshly ground black pepper

pinch of nutmeg

**FOR THE CHEESE AND OLIVE STRAWS**

1 packet ready-rolled puff pastry

50 g (2 oz) pitted black olives

50 g (2 oz/1/2 cup) grated Parmesan

1 egg yolk

**EQUIPMENT**

food processor

pastry brush

earthenware or pottery fondue set

**METHOD**

Pre-heat the oven to 200°C/400°F/Gas Mark 6.

Make the cheese and olive straws first. Purée the olives in a food processor. Spread the resulting paste over half the pastry.

Sprinkle with Parmesan, then fold the other pastry half on top and press firmly down.

Cut into 13 x 2.5-cm (5 x 1-in) strips, brush with egg yolk and sprinkle with the remaining Parmesan.

Holding both ends of the pastry strips, twist to make a spiral shape. Bake for 10 minutes, or until golden brown. Remove and cool on a rack. These will last for 2 weeks in an airtight container. You can freeze the uncooked spirals for a month.

To make the fondue, rub a non-stick saucepan with half of the cut clove of garlic. Discard the garlic, pour in the wine and bring to a simmer over low heat (do not boil). Gradually stir in the cheese cubes. Mix the kirsch with the cornflour and add to the melted cheese mixture. Taste and season, then add a pinch of nutmeg; stir and simmer.

Rub an earthenware fondue pot with the remaining half garlic clove, then discard the garlic. Pour in the fondue mixture and keep it bubbling gently over a very low heat.

Accompany with kirsch, white wine or beer, and serve with the cheese and olive straws for hand-dipping.

**GRIDDLED CIABATTA ON ROSEMARY SKEWERS** serves 6 **INGREDIENTS** 1 ciabatta loaf; 2 cloves garlic; 125 ml (4 fl oz/$^1$/$_2$ cup) olive oil; salt and freshly ground pepper; 2 sprigs rosemary, made into skewers **METHOD** Cut the ciabatta into 1-cm ($^1$/$_2$-in) slices. Whiz the garlic and rosemary in a food processor, transfer to a small bowl and add the olive oil. Season with salt and pepper. Pour the mixture over the ciabatta slices and leave to marinate for 3 hours. Pre-heat a griddle and, when really hot, griddle the ciabatta until brown on both sides. Cut into chunks, thread on to rosemary sprig skewers and dip into the cheese fondue.

**OLIVE AND PINE NUT BISCOTTI** serves 6 **INGREDIENTS** 250 g (8$^1$/$_2$ oz/1$^3$/$_4$ cups) plain (all-purpose) flour; 150 g (5 oz) black olives, chopped; 150 g (5 oz/1$^1$/$_4$ cups) toasted pine nuts; 1 tsp baking powder; $^1$/$_2$ tsp salt; 4 egg yolks **METHOD** Mix the flour, olives, pine nuts, baking powder and salt together in a bowl. Make a well in the mixture and add the egg yolks. Knead the mixture to a stiff dough, then turn out on to a floured surface. Roll the dough into a ball, cut it in half, then roll both halves into long sausage shapes. Squash the dough down slightly. Bake at 180°C/350°F/Gas Mark 4 for 25-30 minutes. Tap the bottom of the loaf: if it sounds hollow, it is cooked. Let cool on a wire rack, then cut into 1-cm ($^1$/$_2$-in) slices and toast on both sides. Skewer the biscotti and dip into the cheese fondue.

**POTATO WEDGES** serves 6 **INGREDIENTS** 12 medium waxy potatoes; 2 tbsp seasoned flour; olive oil for drizzling **METHOD** Pre-heat the oven to 240°C/475°F/Gas Mark 9. Quarter the potatoes, then place them in a pan of boiling water and bring to the boil. Take out and sprinkle with seasoned flour. Cook in the oven for 45 minutes, or until crispy and brown. If you are making these to eat later, simply re-heat them for 10 minutes at 180°C/350°F/Gas Mark 4 before serving. Arrange on skewers and dip into the cheese fondue.

**PURPLE SPROUTING BROCCOLI** serves 6 **INGREDIENTS** 225 ml (8 fl oz/1 cup) water; 1 vegetable stock cube; 1 tsp marmite or yeast extract; 450 g (1 lb) purple sprouting broccoli; 25 g (1 oz/$^1$/$_4$ cup) toasted, flaked almonds **METHOD** Bring the water to the boil in a saucepan. Dissolve the stock cube in the water, together with the marmite or yeast extract. Add the broccoli, cover, and cook for 2 minutes, or until it is just cooked – it should retain some crispness. Dip the broccoli into the cheese fondue, then sprinkle the cheesy broccoli with toasted almonds.

# SPICY CHEESE FONDUE

serves 6

**INGREDIENTS**

2 tbsp chilli oil

1 red onion, diced

1 red pepper, diced

3 jalapeño chillies, roughly chopped

2 tsp paprika

1 tbsp ground cumin

300 ml (10 fl oz/1$^{1}/_{4}$ cups) lager

juice of $^{1}/_{2}$ lime

150 g (5 oz) cream cheese

450 g (1 lb/4$^{3}/_{4}$ cups) Cheddar or
    other hard cheese, grated

3 avocados, cut into chunks

1 bag tortilla chips or 4 flour tortillas,
    cut into strips

**FOR THE SALSA**

4 plum tomatoes, deseeded and
    diced

$^{1}/_{2}$ red chilli, diced

juice of 1 lemon

2 tbsp chopped coriander (cilantro)

1 red onion, diced

salt and freshly ground pepper

**EQUIPMENT**

cheese grater

lemon juicer

earthenware or pottery fondue set

**METHOD**

Mix all of the salsa ingredients together. Taste and season, then set aside. The salsa can be made a day in advance
and stored in the refrigerator.

Pour the chilli oil into a non-stick saucepan. Add the onion, red pepper and chopped chillies and heat to gently soften
in the chilli oil. Add the paprika and cumin.

After a minute, add the lager and lime juice, allow to simmer, then add the cream cheese and three-quarters of the
grated cheese. Make sure you keep the mixture on a low heat until the cheese has melted. Taste and season.

Transfer the cheese fondue to a fondue pot and keep the heat on low, letting the fondue bubble gently.

Sprinkle the last quarter of the grated cheese over the top of the fondue.

Skewer the avocado chunks and dip them, along with the tortilla chips, into the fondue, then top with a little salsa.

If you are using tortilla strips, simply roll them up, skewer, and dip them into the fondue, followed by the salsa.

# WELSH RAREBIT FONDUE

serves 6

**INGREDIENTS**

15 g ($^3/_4$ oz/1 tbsp) butter

8 rashers rindless streaky bacon, diced

1 onion, diced

3 leeks, diced

350 ml (12 fl oz/1$^1/_2$ cups) light ale

225 g (8 oz/2$^1/_2$ cups) grated
   Caerphilly or medium-strong
   Cheddar cheese

125 g (4 oz/1$^1/_4$ cups) grated strong
   Cheddar cheese

2 tbsp milk

1 tbsp cornflour

1 tsp Dijon mustard

1 tsp Worcestershire sauce

pinch of smoked paprika

salt and freshly ground pepper

sprig of thyme

10 thick slices of white toast, cut into
   chunky cubes with the crusts left on

**EQUIPMENT**

cheese grater

earthenware or pottery fondue set

**METHOD**

Melt the butter in a saucepan and add the bacon, onion and leeks.

Cook until the onion and leeks have softened, then add the ale. Gently bring to the boil to burn off the alcohol.

Carefully add the cheeses to the saucepan and stir until melted.

Mix the milk and cornflour together and add to the cheese mixture. Add the mustard, Worcestershire sauce, paprika, salt and freshly ground pepper.

Taste to ensure that the flour is properly cooked into the mixture.

Transfer the cheese fondue to the fondue pot. Turn the heat on low so that the fondue bubbles gently, then sprinkle the thyme leaves over to garnish. Skewer the chunky toast cubes and dip into the fondue.

# BLUE CHEESE FONDUE

serves 6

**INGREDIENTS**

50 ml (2 fl oz/$^1/_4$ cup) dry white wine

225 g (8 oz) cream cheese, broken up

225 g (8 oz/2$^1/_2$ cups) Cheddar or
     Monterey Jack cheese, cubed

125 g (4 oz/1$^1/_4$ cups) blue cheese,
     e.g. Stilton, crumbled

1 tbsp kirsch

2 pears, cut into chunks

1 apple, cut into thick slices

1 head celery, cleaned and cut into
     sticks

1 loaf walnut bread, cut into chunks

**EQUIPMENT**

earthenware or pottery fondue set

**METHOD**

Heat the wine and cream cheese in a non-stick saucepan, stirring until the cheese melts.

Slowly add the Cheddar cheese, stirring constantly, then add the blue cheese. When the mixture is smooth, add the kirsch. Taste and season.

Transfer the cheese fondue to an earthenware or pottery fondue pot and allow to bubble gently over a low heat.

Hand-dip pieces of pear and apple, along with celery sticks, into the fondue, and skewer and dip chunks of the walnut bread.

# GREEN FONDUE

serves 6

**INGREDIENTS**

1 clove garlic

250 ml (8 fl oz/1 cup) medium-dry
white wine

1 lemon, juiced

675 g (1$^1$/$_2$ lb/7$^1$/$_4$ cups) Edam or
Gouda cheese cut into small
chunks

1 tbsp corn flour

1 tbsp water

250 ml (1 cup) chopped
flat-leaf parsley

3 tbsp finely chopped chives

2 tbsp roughly chopped tarragon

3 tbsp of gin

salt and freshly ground pepper

28 g (1 oz/1$^1$/$_4$ cups) butter

3 courgettes (zucchini), cut into thick
batons

3 red peppers, cut into thick strips

18 spears of baby corn

**EQUIPMENT**

lemon juicer

earthenware or pottery fondue set

**METHOD**

Rub the sides and bottom of a saucepan with the garlic clove. Add the wine and bring just to the boil, then add the
lemon juice and turn the heat down very low.

Add the cubes of cheese slowly, stirring continuously until all the cheese has melted. Mix the corn flour with the
water and add to the melted cheese pot.

Turn up the heat and cook for about 3 minutes, until the cheese becomes thick.

Lower the heat again and add the herbs and gin. Season to taste. Cook for another 5 minutes.

Transfer the cheese fondue to a fondue pot and heat on low to warm gently.

Melt the butter in a frying pan and toss the vegetables until they become slightly brown.

Hand-dip or skewer and dip the vegetables into the fondue.

# NEW YORK FONDUE

serves 6

**INGREDIENTS**

450 g (1 lb) full-fat cream cheese

225 ml (8 fl oz/1 cup) full-cream milk

125 g (4 oz) smoked salmon, diced

1 tbsp creamed horseradish

3 tbsp chopped dill

salt and freshly ground pepper

24 mini bagels or 8 full-sized bagels,
    halved and toasted

**EQUIPMENT**

earthenware or pottery fondue set

**METHOD**

Mix the cream cheese and milk together in a saucepan and stir over a medium heat until smooth.

Transfer the cheese fondue to the fondue pot and add the smoked salmon, horseradish and dill.

Turn the heat on low – if it is too high it will cook the salmon. Taste and season.

Skewer the toasted bagels and dip away!

# STOCK FONDUES

## PRAWN AND CHIVE DUMPLINGS WITH SOY SAUCE

serves 6

**INGREDIENTS**

**FOR THE STOCK**

600 ml (1 pt/2$^1$/$_2$ cups) water

4 lemongrass stalks, sliced diagonally

1 small piece ginger, peeled and sliced

1 bunch spring onions, sliced diagonally

3 lime leaves, roughly torn

3 red chillies, thinly sliced diagonally

2 tins coconut milk

1 tbsp fish sauce

2 tbsp oyster sauce

**FOR THE DUMPLINGS**

450 g (1 lb) prawns, cooked and
   peeled

1 tsp sesame oil

2 cloves garlic, crushed

1 bunch chives, finely chopped

squeeze of lemon juice

salt and freshly ground pepper

3 spring onions, finely chopped

40 g (1$^1$/$_2$ oz/$^3$/$_4$ cup) white
   breadcrumbs

36 round sheets dumpling pastry

**EQUIPMENT**

food processor

pastry brush

garlic crusher

lemon juicer

individual mini sieves

cast iron or stainless steel fondue set

**METHOD**

Make the stock a day in advance. Gently simmer the stock ingredients in a saucepan for an hour. Refrigerate until needed.

To make the dumplings, mix all the ingredients, except the pastry sheets and breadcrumbs, in a food processor to a chunky consistency. Fold in the breadcrumbs to make a drier mixture and check the seasoning.

Dust a work surface with flour and lay out the pastry sheets. Using a pastry brush, brush around the edges of the pastry with water, then place a heaped teaspoon of the mixture in the centre of each circle. Bring the edges of the pastry together to form a semi-circle and make three pinches, equal distances apart, around the edge.

Transfer the stock to a fondue pot and simmer, then lower in the dumplings. Cook until they become translucent and float to the surface. Lift out the dumplings with the sieves, garnish with spring onions and serve with soy sauce for dipping.

**SHIITAKE MUSHROOMS WITH LEMON SOY DIP** serves 6 **INGREDIENTS** 225 g (8 oz) shiitake mushrooms, sliced into bite-sized pieces; juice of 1 lemon; 450 ml (16 fl oz/2 cups) light soy sauce; fish stock (see page 31) **METHOD** To make the dip, add the lemon juice to the soy sauce. Place the fish stock in a fondue pot and simmer. Pop the mushrooms into the simmering stock fondue for a few minutes and heat them until they are soft. Serve with the lemon soy dip.

**PRAWNS WITH CUCUMBER AND MINT SALSA** serves 6 **INGREDIENTS** 32 uncooked king prawns, shelled and de-veined; 1 cucumber, peeled, deseeded and diced; 1 red onion, diced; 3 tbsp chopped fresh mint; $1/2$ red chilli, chopped; 1 tbsp white wine vinegar; $1^1/_2$ tsp olive oil; $1^1/_2$ tsp sugar; fish stock (see page 31) **METHOD** For the salsa, mix all the ingredients together except for the prawns and stock. Taste, season and leave for 1 hour. Place the stock in a fondue pot and simmer. Skewer the prawns and cook in the stock fondue until they turn from translucent to pink. Serve with the salsa.

**LIME CHICKEN WITH A COCONUT DIP** serves 6 **INGREDIENTS** 2 lime leaves, roughly torn; 1 tin coconut milk; 1 chicken stock cube dissolved in 1 tbsp hot water; 6 chicken breasts; 4 limes; fish stock (see page 31) **METHOD** Put the lime leaves, coconut milk and chicken stock in a saucepan and bring just to the boil. Set aside. Cut the chicken into cubes. Take a lime quarter and thread it on to a skewer, followed by a cube of chicken, then a piece of lime, finishing with a piece of chicken. Place the fish stock in a fondue pot and simmer. Cook the chicken and lime skewers in the stock fondue for 5 minutes, or until the chicken is cooked through. Serve with the cold coconut dip.

**MONKFISH WITH SWEET SOY DIP** serves 6 **INGREDIENTS** 900 g (2 lb) monkfish, trimmed and cut into cubes; salt and freshly ground pepper; 4 red peppers, cut into chunks; fish stock (see page 31) **FOR THE SWEET SOY DIP** 200 g (7 oz/1 cup) caster (superfine) sugar; 700 ml ($1^1/_4$ pt/3 cups) water; 2 tbsp soy sauce **METHOD** To make the sweet soy dip, place the sugar and water in a saucepan and boil until the mixture begins to thicken (about 5 minutes). Add the soy sauce and leave to cool. Season the monkfish. Thread the monkfish cubes and pepper chunks alternately on to skewers. Place the fish stock in a fondue pot and simmer. Lower the skewers into the stock fondue and cook for 5 minutes. Serve with the soy dip.

# SPINACH AND RICOTTA TORTELLINI WITH NAPOLETANA SAUCE

serves 6

**INGREDIENTS**

2 x 500 g (1 lb) packets spinach and
   ricotta tortellini

**FOR THE STOCK**

2 bay leaves

1 bottle white wine

4 celery sticks

1 sprig fresh lemon thyme

10 peppercorns

450 ml (16 fl oz/2 cups) sherry or
   Marsala

1½ pt (3½ cups) strong chicken
   stock

4 lemon slices

**FOR THE NAPOLETANA SAUCE**

4 cloves garlic, crushed

4 tbsp olive oil

2 x 410 g (14 oz) tins plum tomatoes

1 bay leaf

2 tsp fresh chopped oregano

1 tsp honey

salt and freshly ground pepper

**EQUIPMENT**

garlic crusher

large stockpot

cast iron or stainless steel fondue set

**METHOD**

Make the stock 1–3 days in advance. Place all ingredients into a large stockpot and bring to the boil, then gently simmer for 1 hour. Taste and season. Cool and refrigerate.

To make the Napoletana sauce, sauté the garlic in olive oil until brown, then add the tomatoes, bay leaf and oregano. Reduce the heat, simmer for 20 minutes, then add the honey. Taste and season.

Transfer the stock to a fondue pot and bring to the boil, then turn down the heat to a gentle simmer. Skewer the tortellini and cook in the fondue for 10 minutes, or as instructed on the packet. Dip into the Napoletana sauce.

Variation: **CHICKEN AND BASIL WITH PESTO DIP** serves 6 **INGREDIENTS** 4 skinless, boneless chicken breasts, cut into 6 strips. For the marinade: 1 bunch fresh basil; drizzle of olive oil. For the pesto dip: 1 bunch fresh basil; 4 cloves garlic; 150 g (5 oz/1½ cups) grated Parmesan; 2 tbsp pine nuts; 200 ml (7 fl oz/¾ cup) olive oil; salt and freshly ground pepper **METHOD** To make the marinade, put the basil and olive oil in the blender and whizz until smooth and dry. Pour over the chicken and leave for at least 1 hour. Blend the ingredients for the pesto until nearly smooth. Transfer the stock to a fondue pot and bring to the boil, then turn down to a gentle simmer. Skewer the marinated chicken and cook in the stock fondue for 5–8 minutes. Serve with the pesto dip.

# BACCHUS WITH BEEF FILLET AND RED ONION MARMALADE

serves 6

**INGREDIENTS**

900 g (2 lb) beef fillet, cut into 2.5-cm
(1-in) cubes

**FOR THE BACCHUS**

900 ml (1¹/₂ pt/3³/₄ cups) strong
chicken stock

900 ml (1¹/₂ pt/3³/₄ cups) red wine

1 onion, thinly sliced

3 celery sticks, roughly chopped

1 clove garlic, roughly chopped

8 juniper berries, crushed

10 peppercorns, crushed

salt and freshly ground pepper

1 tbsp chopped fresh tarragon or
1 tsp, dried

2 sprigs fresh thyme or ¹/₂ tsp, dried

2 sprigs fresh parsley

1 bay leaf

**FOR THE MARMALADE**

25 g (1 oz) butter

5 red onions, halved and finely sliced

1 tbsp soft light-brown sugar

250 ml (9 fl oz/1 cup) red wine

55 ml (2 fl oz/¹/₄ cup) red wine
vinegar

salt and freshly ground black pepper

**EQUIPMENT**

pestle and mortar

fine sieve

cast iron or stainless steel fondue set

**METHOD**

Make the Bacchus at least one day in advance. Bring the stock and wine to the boil in a stockpot. Combine the remaining ingredients and add to the mixture. Bring to the boil again. Cool, then refrigerate.

To make the marmalade, melt the butter in a non-stick saucepan and add the onions and sugar.

Cook until soft and lightly caramelised.

Add the wine and vinegar and cook for about 20 minutes, or until all the liquid has evaporated and the onions are soft.

Season with salt and freshly ground pepper.

Just before serving, strain the Bacchus mixture through a fine sieve. Bring to the boil, pour into a fondue pot and place over a heater so that the Bacchus fondue simmers slowly.

Thread the beef cubes on to skewers and cook to taste in the Bacchus. Serve with the red onion marmalade.

# OIL FONDUES

serves 6

**INGREDIENTS**

1.1 L (2 pt/4$^3$/$_4$ cups) vegetable oil

2 red chillies, sliced

**FOR THE TEMPURA**

2 under-ripe avocados, peeled and cut
   into thick slices

2 sweet potatoes, peeled and cut into
   thick slices

2 red peppers, deseeded and cut into
   thick slices

2 packets baby corn

16 broccoli florets

125 g (4 oz/$^3$/$_4$ cup) plain
   (all-purpose flour)

1 egg

225 ml (8 fl oz/1 cup) iced water

**FOR THE WASABI MAYONNAISE**

4 tbsp mayonnaise

1 tsp wasabi paste

1 tbsp light soy sauce

squeeze of lemon juice

**EQUIPMENT**

sieve

funnel

glass bottle

whisk

cast iron or stainless steel fondue set

**METHOD**

To make the fondue oil, heat the vegetable oil gently in a large, heavy-based saucepan and add the chillies.

Cook for about 10 minutes on low heat, or longer for spicier oil.

Allow to cool, leaving the chillies in the oil. When cold, strain the oil and pour through a funnel into a bottle.

Mix all the wasabi mayonnaise ingredients together in a bowl; taste and season.

Make up the tempura batter, making sure you keep the mixture cold. Break the egg into the flour and whisk slowly, adding

the chilled water. The batter should coat the back of a spoon and resemble pancake batter in consistency.

Transfer the chilli oil to a fondue pot and adjust to medium heat.

Coat the vegetables in the batter, thread them onto skewers and fry in the hot chilli oil fondue.

Drain and serve the tempura with the wasabi mayonnaise dip.

# MOROCCAN LAMB WITH TOMATO-APRICOT SAUCE

serves 6

**INGREDIENTS**

1.1 L (2 pt/4$^3$/$_4$ cups) vegetable oil

10 cloves garlic, peeled and sliced

**FOR THE LAMB**

4 lamb fillets, 900 g (2 lb) total weight

2 cloves garlic

1 tbsp cumin seeds

1 tsp chilli powder

**FOR THE SAUCE**

oil for frying

1 tbsp cumin seeds

1 large onion, finely diced

1 x 400 g (14 oz) tin chopped
    tomatoes

50 g (2 oz/$^1$/$_3$ cup) dried apricots,
    finely chopped

salt and freshly ground pepper

**EQUIPMENT**

sieve

funnel

glass bottle

food processor

pestle and mortar

cast iron or stainless steel fondue set

**METHOD**

To make the fondue oil, gently heat the vegetable oil in a saucepan and add the garlic, keeping the temperature low. Let the garlic cook in the oil for about 10 minutes. Cool, leaving the garlic in the oil.

When cold, strain the oil and pour through a funnel into a bottle.

Slice the lamb fillets into 1-cm ($^1$/$_2$-in)-thick medallions.

In a food processor, combine the garlic, 1 tbsp of cumin seeds and 1 tsp of chilli powder and smooth the mixture over the fillets. Leave for 1 hour or up to 1 day.

To make the sauce, crush the cumin seeds using a pestle and mortar and fry in a little oil. Add the onion and fry until soft, then add the chopped tomatoes and apricots. Season.

Transfer the garlic oil into a fondue pot and adjust to medium heat.

Thread the marinated lamb medallions on to skewers and fry in the hot garlic oil fondue for a minute or longer, depending on how you like your meat cooked. Dip into the tomato-apricot sauce.

**CHICKEN SATAY SERVED WITH PEANUT DIP AND ROLLED IN CRISPY VERMICELLI** serves 6 **INGREDIENTS** 4 tbsp smooth peanut butter; boiling water; 2 tsp sweet chilli sauce; 85 g (3 oz/$^3/_4$ cup) crispy vermicelli; 6 skinless, boneless chicken breasts, cut into 5-cm (2-in) rectangles; garlic oil (see page 41) **METHOD** Put the peanut butter in a bowl and slowly add boiling water until a loose paste is formed. Add the chilli sauce. Put the vermicelli in a bowl. Transfer the garlic oil to a fondue pot and adjust to medium heat. Skewer the chicken and cook in the garlic oil fondue for 3 minutes, or until cooked through. Dip the chicken into the peanut dip and roll in the vermicelli. Eat immediately (or the vermicelli will go soggy).

**CHICKEN GOUJONS WITH GARLIC AND CHIVE BUTTER** serves 6 **INGREDIENTS** 6 skinless, boneless chicken breasts; 2 eggs; 50 g (2 oz/$^1/_3$ cup) seasoned flour; 85 g (3 oz/$^1/_2$ cup) matzo meal; 125 g (4 oz/$^1/_2$ cup) butter; 3 cloves garlic, crushed; 1 packet chives, finely chopped; garlic oil (see page 41) **METHOD** Cut the chicken breasts into spears. Beat the eggs in a bowl. Put the flour and matzo meal into two separate bowls. Coat the chicken in the flour, dip in the egg, and then in the matzo meal. Skewer the coated chicken. Melt the butter, remove from heat and add the garlic and chives. Transfer the garlic oil to a fondue pot and adjust to medium heat. Cook the chicken in the fondue for 3 minutes, or until cooked through. Dip into the chive butter.

**BEEF FILLET WITH HORSERADISH MAYONNAISE** **INGREDIENTS** 225 ml (8 fl oz/1 cup) mayonnaise; 2.5-cm (1-in) piece fresh horseradish, grated, or 1 tbsp creamed horseradish; 900 g (2 lb) beef fillet, cut into 5-cm (2-in) rectangles; salt and freshly ground pepper; garlic oil (see page 41) **METHOD** Mix the mayonnaise and the horseradish together. Season the beef and thread it on to skewers. Transfer the garlic oil to a fondue pot and adjust to medium heat. Cook the beef in the garlic oil fondue for 1-2 minutes, or until cooked to taste. Dip into the horseradish mayonnaise.

**MARINATED DUCK BREAST WITH MANGO SALSA** **INGREDIENTS** 4 duck breasts, cut into 1-cm ($^1/_2$-in) slices; 1 red onion, finely diced; 4 spring onions, finely chopped; 1 mango, finely diced; $^1/_2$ red chilli, finely chopped; 1 small bunch fresh coriander (cilantro), roughly chopped; salt and freshly ground pepper; garlic oil (see page 41) **METHOD** Mix all the salsa ingredients together and season. Leave for 1 hour. Transfer the garlic oil to a fondue pot and adjust to medium heat. Thread the duck slices on to skewers and cook in the garlic oil fondue for 2 minutes, or until cooked to taste. Serve with the mango salsa.

# CURRIED SWORDFISH WITH SPICY GREEN SAUCE

serves 6

**INGREDIENTS**

1.1 L (2 pt/4³/₄ cups) peanut oil

900 g (2 lb) swordfish, cut into chunks

**FOR THE MARINADE**

1 tbsp mild curry paste

juice of 1 lemon

1 tbsp water

2 green chillies, finely chopped

2.5-cm (1-in) piece root ginger

**FOR THE SPICY GREEN SAUCE**

1 bunch fresh coriander (cilantro)

5 tbsp cumin seeds

pinch of white salt

pinch of freshly ground black pepper

1 tsp sugar

juice of half a lemon

1–2 small green chillies, finely chopped

3 ripe tomatoes, skinned and
   deseeded

**EQUIPMENT**

lemon juicer

food processor

fine sieve

cast iron or stainless steel fondue set

**METHOD**

To make the marinade, mix the curry paste, water, lemon juice, chopped chillies and ginger together in a food processor and coat the swordfish chunks with the mixture. Leave for at least 1 hour.

To make the sauce, in a small food processor chop the coriander (cilantro) leaves and stalks and blend in the cumin seeds, salt, pepper, sugar and lemon juice. Once blended, add the chopped chilli to taste, a little at a time. Chop the tomato into small squares and add to the sauce. Pour the peanut oil into a fondue pot and adjust to medium heat. Skewer the fish and fry in the peanut oil fondue for 3 minutes, or until cooked. Serve with the warm spicy green sauce.

Variation: **SALT AND PEPPER SQUID WITH SWEET CHILLI SAUCE** serves 6 **INGREDIENTS** 900 g (2 lb) squid or octopus, gutted and cleaned; 2 tsp flaked sea salt; 2 tsp freshly ground pepper; 125 g (4 oz/³/₄ cup) plain (all-purpose) flour; 225 ml (8 fl oz) sweet chilli sauce **METHOD** Take the squid and, keeping the body whole, slice into 1-cm (¹/₂-in) pieces to make rings. Mix the sea salt and pepper together with the flour. One ring at a time, coat the squid in the flour, dusting off any excess. Transfer the peanut oil to a fondue pot and adjust to medium heat. Thread the squid rings on to skewers and fry in the peanut oil fondue for 2 minutes, or until cooked through (do not overcook or the squid will become rubbery). Serve with the sweet chilli sauce.

# FISH IN BEER BATTER WITH TARTARE SAUCE, AND CHUNKY CHIPS WITH SWEET CHILLI AND SOUR CREAM DIP

serves 6

**INGREDIENTS**

1.1 L (2 pt/4³/₄ cups) vegetable oil

550 g (1¹/₄ lb) skinless, boneless
    cod, cut into chunks

1 lemon, cut into 6 wedges

**FOR THE BATTER**

125 g (4 oz/1 cup) plain (all-purpose)
    flour

pinch of baking powder

1 egg yolk

100 ml (3¹/₂ fl oz/¹/₂ cup) ale

salt and freshly ground pepper

**FOR THE CHIPS**

900 g (2 lb) red potatoes

oil for frying

225 ml (8 fl oz/1 cup) sour cream

225 ml (8 fl oz) sweet chilli sauce

**FOR THE TARTARE SAUCE**

450 ml (16 fl oz) mayonnaise

1 tbsp capers

1 tsp gherkins, roughly chopped

1 bunch fresh parsley, chopped

1 tbsp lemon juice

2 tbsp spring onion, chopped

**EQUIPMENT**

whisk

heavy-based saucepan for deep-frying

cast iron or stainless steel fondue set

**METHOD**

Make the batter by whisking the flour, baking powder, egg yolk and ale together. Season the batter and leave to stand for 1 hour, after which time the consistency should be thick.

To make the chips, peel and cut the potatoes into wedges. Place the wedges in a saucepan filled with cold, salted water and bring to the boil. Drain and dry the wedges. Heat some oil and deep-fry the chips in a heavy-based saucepan for about 10 minutes, or until golden brown. Keep hot in the oven.

Mix all the tartare sauce ingredients together and place in a bowl. Put aside.

Transfer the vegetable oil to a fondue pot and adjust the heat to medium.

Thread the cod on to skewers, dip into the batter and carefully fry in the vegetable oil fondue until cooked through, or until brown. Drain on kitchen paper (paper towel). Squeeze lemon juice over the battered fish and serve with the tartare sauce for dipping. Pour the sour cream into a bowl, make a well and pour the chilli sauce in the centre. Dip the chunky chips.

**TUNA AND COURGETTE (ZUCCHINI) SKEWERS WITH QUICK AIOLI** serves 6 **INGREDIENTS** 900 g (2 lb) fresh tuna, cut into chunks; 2 courgettes (zucchini), cut into 1-cm ($^3/_8$-in) rounds; 1 egg, beaten; 125 g (4 oz/1 cup) seasoned flour **FOR THE AIOLI** 225 ml (8 fl oz) mayonnaise; 1 tsp Dijon mustard; juice of 1 lemon; 1 clove garlic, crushed; salt and freshly ground pepper **METHOD** To make the aïoli, mix the mayonnaise with the mustard, lemon juice and garlic. Taste and season. Dip the courgette (zucchini) rounds in the beaten egg, then roll them in the flour. Thread the courgette (zucchini) rounds and tuna chunks alternately on to skewers. Transfer the vegetable oil to a fondue pot and adjust the heat to medium. Cook the courgette (zucchini) and tuna skewers in the vegetable oil fondue for 2 minutes – the tuna should still be pink in the middle (if you prefer it cooked through, cook for longer). Serve with the aïoli for dipping.

**MONKFISH WRAPPED IN PARMA HAM WITH PEA PESTO** serves 6 **INGREDIENTS** 900 g (2 lb) skinless, boneless monkfish, cut into chunks; 18 slices Parma ham; 36 large basil leaves **FOR THE PEA PESTO** 225 g (8 oz) peas; 2 cloves garlic; 50 g (2 oz/$^1/_2$ cup) grated Parmesan; 1 tbsp toasted pine nuts; 125 ml (4 fl oz/$^1/_2$ cup) olive oil; salt and freshly ground pepper **METHOD** Cook the peas and refresh in cold water. Put the peas, garlic, Parmesan and pine nuts in a food processor. Whizz, adding half the oil slowly until you have a thick but fluid pesto. Taste and season. Lay out the ham slices and cut each in half from top to bottom. Put a basil leaf in the centre of each piece, then lay the monkfish on top. Fold in the edges of the ham to cover the monkfish. Skewer to secure. Transfer the vegetable oil to a fondue pot and adjust the heat to medium. Fry the skewered ham and fish in the vegetable oil fondue for 2 minutes – the ham will go crispy. Dip into the pea pesto.

**SPRING ROLLS WITH PLUM SAUCE** serves 6 **INGREDIENTS** 12 spring roll wrappers; 2 egg whites; 1 jar of plum sauce **FOR THE FILLING** 1 onion, finely chopped; 1 red chilli, finely diced; 1 clove garlic, finely diced; 1 carrot, peeled and grated; 50 g (2 oz) bean sprouts; 1 black fungus mushroom, soaked and finely sliced; 2 shiitake mushrooms, finely sliced; 50 g (2 oz) thin rice noodles, soaked; 200 g (7 oz) pork mince; 125 g (4 oz) uncooked prawns, roughly chopped **METHOD** Mix all the ingredients for the filling together except for the prawns. Taste and season. Lay out the spring roll wrappers with the corner points facing you and divide the filling mixture between the sheets, placing it slightly off centre and in a cigar shape. Divide the prawns between the sheets, placing them on top of each mound of cigar-shaped filling. Brush all the way round the wrapper with egg white. Fold the bottom point of the wrapper over the mixture. Press down. Fold both sides in. Roll up the rest of the wrapper tightly. Transfer the vegetable oil to a fondue pot and adjust the heat to medium. Skewer the spring rolls and fry for 3 minutes in the vegetable oil fondue. Serve with the plum sauce.

# LIME-MARINATED SCALLOPS WITH COCONUT-SESAME DIP

serves 6

**INGREDIENTS**

36 scallops with their red corals on
and muscles removed

grated rind and juice of 4 limes

salt and freshly ground pepper

1 tin coconut cream or 150 ml
(5 fl oz/$^2$/$_3$ cup) carton coconut
cream

3 tbsp sesame oil

1.1 L (2 pt/4$^3$/$_4$ cups) coconut oil

**EQUIPMENT**

lemon zester

lemon squeezer

cast iron or stainless steel fondue set

**METHOD**

Marinate the scallops in half the lime juice and all the rind, salt and freshly ground pepper.

To make the dip, mix the coconut cream with the remaining lime juice, then drip the sesame oil into the

centre of the coconut cream mixture.

Transfer the coconut oil to a fondue pot and adjust the heat to medium.

Thread the scallops on to skewers and cook in the coconut oil fondue for about 2 minutes (do not overcook or

the scallops will become rubbery). Dip into the coconut-sesame dip.

Variation: **GARLIC PRAWNS WITH A GINGER, SOY AND SESAME DIP** serves 6 **INGREDIENTS**

36 raw king prawns, tails off but shells on; 3 cloves garlic, crushed; 225 ml (8 fl oz/1 cup) light soy

sauce; 1 tbsp toasted sesame seeds; 1 tsp stem ginger juice **METHOD** Coat the prawns in

garlic and leave for 1 hour. To make the dip, mix together the soy sauce, sesame seeds and ginger

juice. Transfer the coconut oil to a fondue pot and adjust the heat to medium. Thread the prawns on

to skewers and cook in the coconut oil fondue for 3-4 minutes. Serve with the ginger, soy and sesame dip.

# FILLET OF BEEF WITH BOURGUIGNONNE DIP

Serves 6

**INGREDIENTS**

1.1 L (2 pt/4$^3$/$_4$ cups) peanut oil

700 g (1$^1$/$_2$ lb) beef fillet, cut into
  thick strips

**FOR THE MARINADE**

$^1$/$_2$ bottle red Burgundy wine

1 onion, finely diced

2 cloves garlic, crushed

2 bay leaves

1 tbsp lemon thyme

1 small bunch fresh flat-leaf parsley

salt and freshly ground pepper

**EQUIPMENT**

cast iron or stainless steel fondue set

**METHOD**

Mix all the marinade ingredients together and pour over the beef. Leave for at least 1 hour.

To make the dip, remove the beef from the marinade and reduce the remainder of the marinade in a saucepan until thick.

Transfer the peanut oil to a fondue pot and adjust the heat to medium.

Thread the beef on to skewers and cook for 1 minute in the hot oil fondue (or longer if you prefer your meat well-cooked). Serve with the reduced marinade as a dip.

# SWEET FONDUES

## DARK CHOCOLATE FONDUE WITH STEM GINGER JUICE

serves 6

**INGREDIENTS**

225 ml (8 fl oz/1 cup) double (heavy) cream

2 tbsp stem ginger juice

25 g (1 oz/$^1/_8$ cup) unsalted butter

300 g (10 oz/1$^3/_4$ cups) plain chocolate

2 oranges, cut into segments

2 Comice pears, cut into segments and cored

6 pieces stem ginger

**EQUIPMENT**

porcelain fondue set

**METHOD**

Gently heat the cream, stem ginger juice, butter and chocolate in a heat-proof bowl over a saucepan of simmering water. Once all the chocolate has melted, transfer to a warmed fondue pot and light the tealight. Dip the fruit into the chocolate fondue by hand, and skewer the ginger for dipping.

Variation: **MILK CHOCOLATE FONDUE WITH ALMOND ROUNDS** Serves 6 **INGREDIENTS** 25 g (1 oz/$^1/_8$ cup) butter; 300 g (10 oz/1$^3/_4$ cups) milk chocolate; 225 ml (8 fl oz/1 cup) double (heavy) cream; 2 tsp amaretto liqueur **FOR THE ALMOND ROUNDS** 170 g (6 oz/1$^1/_4$ cups) ground almonds; 225 g (8 oz/1$^1/_4$ cups) white sugar; $^1/_4$ tsp ground cinnamon; pinch of salt; 2 eggs, one whole and one separated; $^1/_2$ tsp almond extract **METHOD** Pre-heat the oven to 180°C/350°F/Gas Mark 4. Line a baking sheet with baking parchment. Mix the ground almonds, sugar, cinnamon and salt in a food processor. Add a whole egg and an egg white to the almond extract and whizz. Wet your hands and make 2.5-cm (1-in) balls with the mixture. Place on baking parchment and flatten to 5-mm ($^1/_4$-in)-thick rounds. Bake for 12 minutes. To make the chocolate fondue, mix the butter, chocolate, cream and amaretto in a heatproof bowl and place over a saucepan of simmering water. Transfer the melted chocolate to a warmed fondue pot and light the tealight. Skewer the rounds and dip into the chocolate fondue.

## WHITE CHOCOLATE FONDUE WITH CHOCOLATE CHIP BISCOTTI

serves 6 **INGREDIENTS** 225 ml (8 fl oz/1 cup) double (heavy) cream; 25 g (1 oz/$^1/_8$ cup) unsalted butter; 300 g (10 oz/1$^3/_4$ cups) white chocolate **FOR THE BISCOTTI** 225 g (8 oz/1$^1/_2$ cups) plain (all-purpose) flour; 1 tsp baking powder; pinch of salt; 175 g (6 oz/$^3/_4$ cup) caster (superfine) sugar; 100 g (3$^1/_2$ oz/$^3/_4$ cup) flaked almonds, toasted and chopped; 175 g (6 oz/1 cup) chocolate chips; 2 egg yolks; grated rind and juice of 1 lemon **METHOD** Pre-heat the oven to 180°C/350°F/Gas Mark 4. Line a baking sheet with baking parchment. To make the biscotti, mix all the dry ingredients together in a bowl. Make a well at the bottom of the mixture and add the egg yolks and lemon juice. Knead the mixture to a firm dough. On a floured surface, roll the dough into a ball, cut it in half, then roll it into a long sausage shape, about 4 cm (1$^1/_2$ in) in diameter. Flatten until it resembles a ciabatta loaf. Bake in the oven for about 20 minutes and cool on a wire rack. Cut the biscotti into 2.5-cm (1-in) slices, replace on the baking sheet and put in the oven for about 15 minutes, turning when lightly browned. To make the fondue, gently heat the cream, butter and chocolate in a heatproof bowl over a pan of simmering water. Transfer to a warmed fondue pot when melted and light the tealight. Skewer the biscotti and dip into the white chocolate fondue.

## MINT CHOCOLATE FONDUE WITH BROWNIE FINGERS

serves 6 **INGREDIENTS** 225 ml (8 fl oz/1 cup) double (heavy) cream; 25 g (1 oz/$^1/_8$ cup) unsalted butter; 300 g (10 oz/1$^3/_4$ cups) white chocolate; 1 tsp mint essence; 1 tbsp roughly chopped fresh mint **FOR THE BROWNIES** 175 g (6 oz/$^3/_4$ cup) unsalted butter; 175 g (6 oz/1 cup) plain chocolate; 3 eggs; 300 g (10 oz/1$^1/_2$ cups) caster (superfine) sugar; 85 g (3 oz/$^1/_2$ cup) plain (all-purpose) flour; 50 g (2 oz/$^1/_2$ cup) cocoa; 225 g (8 oz/1$^1/_2$ cups) white chocolate, roughly chopped **METHOD** Pre-heat the oven to 180°C/350°F/Gas Mark 4 and line a 25 x 38 cm (10 x 15 in) baking tin with baking parchment. To make the brownies, melt the butter in a saucepan and add the plain chocolate, stirring until it melts. In a bowl whisk the egg and sugar until fluffy, then fold in the chocolate mixture followed by the flour, cocoa and white chocolate. Bake for 40 minutes. Allow to cool, then cut into finger-sized rectangles. To make the fondue, gently heat the cream, butter and chocolate in a heatproof bowl over a saucepan of simmering water. Add the mint essence and the chopped mint. When the chocolate has melted, transfer to a warmed fondue pot and light the tealight. Skewer the brownie fingers and dip into the mint chocolate fondue.

## MARBLED CHOCOLATE FONDUE WITH MINI MARSHMALLOWS

serves 6 **INGREDIENTS** 150 g (5 oz/$^3/_4$ cup) plain chocolate; 150 g (5 oz/$^3/_4$ cup) white chocolate; 225 ml (8 fl oz/1 cup) double (heavy) cream; 25 g (1 oz/$^1/_8$ cup) unsalted butter; 1 bag mini marshmallows **METHOD** To make the fondue, take two pans of water and two heatproof bowls and put the plain chocolate in one bowl and the white in the other. Add half the cream and half the butter to each bowl. Place each heatproof bowl over a saucepan of simmering water and gently melt the chocolate in each bowl. Transfer both types of chocolate to a warmed fondue pot and light the tealight. Carefully whirl the chocolates together with a skewer for a marbled effect. Skewer the pink and yellow marshmallows alternately and dip into the marbled chocolate fondue.

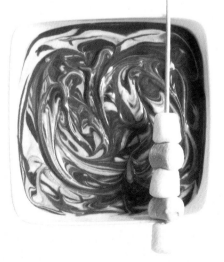

# MARSHMALLOW FONDUE WITH CRISPY CAKES

serves 6

**INGREDIENTS**

600 ml (1 pt/2$^1$/$_2$ cups) double
 (heavy) cream

225 g (8 oz) pink and white
 marshmallows

125 ml (4 fl oz/$^1$/$_2$ cup) raspberry
 coulis

**FOR THE CAKES**

25 g (1 oz/$^1$/$_8$ cup) butter

3 tbsp golden syrup

175 g (6 oz/1 cup) chocolate

225 g (8 oz) cornflake cereal

**EQUIPMENT**

baking parchment

porcelain fondue set

**METHOD**

To make the crispy cakes, line an oven tray with baking parchment.

Melt the butter in a saucepan and add the syrup and chocolate.

Put the cornflakes in a bowl, pour the chocolate syrup over them and mix until all of the cornflakes are coated.

Pour the mixture into an oven tray and place in the refrigerator to set. Once set, cut the crispy cake into circles, squares or rectangles – or a combination of shapes if you wish!

Heat the cream in a saucepan and add the marshmallows and the coulis, stirring until everything has melted.

Pour the marshmallow fondue into a warmed fondue pot and light the tealight.

Hand-dip the crispy cakes into the marshmallow fondue.

# LEMON AND CHAMPAGNE ZABAGLIONE

serves 6

**INGREDIENTS**

600 ml (1 pt/2$^1$/$_2$ cups) champagne

2 eggs

10 egg yolks

400 g (10 oz/1$^1$/$_3$ cups) caster
(superfine) sugar

grated rind of 4 lemons

packet of brioche fingers

packet of lemon biscuits (cookies)

**EQUIPMENT**

metal bowl

whisk

grater

porcelain fondue set

**METHOD**

Place the champagne in a saucepan and reduce by half, then allow to cool.

In a metal bowl whisk the eggs and sugar until they have doubled in volume.

Heat some water in a saucepan until simmering. Place the bowl of whisked egg and sugar over the simmering saucepan and whisk in the champagne and lemon rind. Your goal is to make a thick "custard".

Transfer the custard to a warmed fondue pot and light the tealight.

Serve with lemon biscuits (cookies) and brioche fingers for hand-dipping.

# MULLED WINE FONDUE WITH DRIED FRUITS

serves 6

**INGREDIENTS**

1 bottle burgundy red wine

125 ml (4 fl oz/$1/2$ cup) port

125 ml (4 fl oz/$1/2$ cup) sherry

peeled zest of 1 orange

2 cinnamon sticks

4 star anise

6 cloves

**DRIED FRUITS**

12 dried figs

12 dried apricots

12 pieces of dried mango

**EQUIPMENT**

porcelain fondue set

**METHOD**

Gently heat all the ingredients for the mulled wine fondue in a saucepan and leave to infuse for 3 hours.

The fondue can be made up to 3 days in advance.

Just before serving, pour the mulled wine fondue into a warmed fondue pot and light the tealight.

Skewer the dried fruit and dip in the mulled wine fondue. Leave the skewers in the pot for about 5 minutes, or until the fruit becomes re-hydrated.

# RASPBERRY COCKTAIL WITH BRANDY SNAPS

serves 6

**INGREDIENTS**

900 g (2 lb) fresh or frozen
   raspberries

225 ml (8 fl oz/1 cup) water

100 g ($3^1/_2$ oz/$^1/_2$ cup) caster
   (superfine) sugar

125 ml (4 fl oz/$^1/_2$ cup) cassis

600 ml (1 pt/$2^1/_2$ cups) champagne
   or sparkling wine

**FOR THE BRANDY SNAPS**

50 g (2 oz/$^1/_4$ cup) butter or
   margarine

100 g (3 oz/$^1/_2$ cup) caster
   (superfine) sugar

1 rounded tbsp golden syrup

50 g (2 oz/$^1/_2$ cup) plain (all-purpose)
   flour, sifted

$^1/_2$ tsp ground ginger

**EQUIPMENT**

3 baking trays

3 wooden spoons

baking parchment

sieve

palette knife

**METHOD**

To make the raspberry cocktail, place the raspberries, water and sugar in a saucepan and heat gently for 15 minutes to soften the fruit and dissolve the sugar.

Pour into a sieve and strain the mixture. The mixture should be thick, with no pips.

To make the brandy snaps, pre-heat the oven to 180°C/350°F/Gas Mark 4. Grease 3 baking trays and the handles of 3 wooden spoons.

Place the butter, sugar and syrup in a pan and heat slowly until the butter has melted.

Remove from the heat and stir in the flour and ginger.

Place teaspoonfuls of the mixture on the 3 trays, spacing them 15 cm (6 in) apart. (If you do not have 3 baking trays, bake in batches.) Bake for 8–10 minutes, or until golden brown.

Allow the snaps to cool until just warm, then loosen them with a palette knife. Gently roll the warm, pliable snaps around the spoon handles with the upper surfaces on the outside.

When the snaps have hardened, gently slip them off the spoon handles.

To serve, add the champagne and cassis to the raspberry mixture, pour into a fondue pot and light the tealight to gently reheat. Hand-dip the snaps into the raspberry cocktail.

## BANANA ROUNDS

### INGREDIENTS

6 bananas

2 lemons

### METHOD

Slice the bananas into bite-sized rounds and squeeze some lemon juice over them to stop them from discolouring. Pour the raspberry cocktail into a fondue pot and light the tealight to gently warm. Skewer the bananas and dive in!

## CHOCOLATE TRUFFLES

### INGREDIENTS

50 g (2 oz/$^1/_4$ cup) butter

225 g (8 oz/1$^1/_2$ cups) dark chocolate

150 ml (5 fl oz/$^1/_2$ cup) double (heavy) cream

50 g (2 oz/$^1/_2$ cup) cocoa

### METHOD

Gently melt the butter in a saucepan and add the chocolate and cream, mixing until smooth. Place the mixture in the refrigerator for at least 1 hour, or until the mixture starts to set. With a teaspoon or a melon-baller, scoop out the chocolate and roll it into balls, then drop the balls into the cocoa. Pour the raspberry cocktail into a fondue pot and light the tealight to gently warm. Skewer the truffles and dip them into the raspberry cocktail.

## MINI MERINGUE STICKS

### INGREDIENTS

4 egg whites

300 g (10 oz/1$^1$/$_2$ cups) caster (superfine) sugar

### METHOD

Pre-heat the oven to 110°C/225°F/Gas Mark $^1$/$_4$. Whisk the egg whites until soft peaks form, then gradually add the sugar, whisking each bit of sugar until it has been absorbed. Fill a piping bag with the mixture. Pipe a thin 10 cm (4 in) line, then pipe individual dots down the line, creating a "pearl necklace" effect. Repeat until all of the mixture has been used up. Bake for 1 hour, or until completely hard. Pour the raspberry cocktail into a fondue pot and light the tealight to gently warm. Hand-dip the meringue sticks into the raspberry cocktail.

## CHOCOLATE WAFER CIGARS

### INGREDIENTS

1 box chocolate wafer cigars (about 24 wafer cigars)

### METHOD

Pour the raspberry cocktail into a fondue pot and light the tealight to gently warm. Open the packet of cigars and hand-dunk!

# LEMON CREAM FONDUE WITH VANILLA CHOCOLATE CHIP CAKES

serves 6

**INGREDIENTS**

850 ml (1$^1$/$_2$ pt/3$^1$/$_2$ cups) double (heavy) cream

grated rind and juice of 6 lemons

4 tbsp sherry

50 g (2 oz/$^1$/$_4$ cup) caster (superfine) sugar

**FOR THE VANILLA CAKES**

50 g (2 oz/$^1$/$_4$ cup) caster (superfine) sugar

1 egg

125 ml (4 fl oz/$^1$/$_2$ cup) whole milk

$^1$/$_2$ tsp vanilla paste

50 g (2 oz/$^1$/$_4$ cup) butter, melted

40 g (1$^1$/$_2$ oz/$^1$/$_4$ cup) plain chocolate, chopped into small pieces

35 g (1$^1$/$_4$ oz/$^1$/$_4$ cup) plain (all-purpose) flour

1$^1$/$_2$ tsp baking powder

pinch of salt

**EQUIPMENT**

whisk

30 paper muffin cases or a silicon muffin tin

wire rack

lemon zester

porcelain fondue set

**METHOD**

To make the vanilla chocolate chip cakes, pre-heat the oven to 200°C/400°F/Gas Mark 6.

Whisk the sugar, egg, milk, vanilla paste and butter together in a large bowl.

Put all the remaining ingredients into the bowl and gently fold in.

Drop the mixture into the muffin cases or a muffin tin. Take care not to overfill the cases, as the cakes will rise during baking.

Bake for 10 minutes, or until golden brown. Remove the cakes from the oven and allow to cool on a wire rack. The cakes will keep for about 2 weeks in an airtight container.

To make the lemon cream fondue, mix the cream, grated rind, lemon juice, sherry and caster (superfine) sugar together, keeping a small amount of grated rind aside for the garnish.

Transfer the mixture to a fondue pot and light the tealight to heat very gently.

Hand-dip the cakes into the lemon cream fondue.

## CHOCOLATE CHIP COOKIES serves 6

**INGREDIENTS** 225 g (8 oz/1 cup) butter; 1$^1$/$_2$ tbsp brown sugar; 1 tsp vanilla extract; 2 eggs; 125 g (4 oz/$^3$/$_4$ cup) plain (all-purpose) flour; 125 g (4 oz/$^3$/$_4$ cup) self-raising flour; 50 g (2 oz/$^1$/$_2$ cup) cocoa; 225 g (8 oz/1$^1$/$_2$ cups) plain chocolate, chopped; 50 g (2 oz/$^3$/$_4$ cup) coconut

**METHOD** Pre-heat the oven to 160°C/325°F/Gas Mark 3. Line a baking tray with parchment. Soften the butter and mix in the sugar and vanilla with an electric whisk. Add the eggs and mix. Sift in both types of the flour and the cocoa, then add the chopped chocolate and coconut. Mix well until all the flour is absorbed. Spoon rounds of the mixture on to the baking sheet and bake for about 15 minutes, or until the cookies are hard on the outside and slightly gooey on the inside. Transfer the lemon cream fondue to a fondue pot and light the tealight to heat very gently. Hand-dip the cookies into the lemon cream fondue.

## GINGER THINS serves 6

**INGREDIENTS** 50 g (2 oz/$^1$/$_4$ cup) butter; 125 ml (4 fl oz/$^1$/$_2$ cup) golden syrup; 1 tsp bicarbonate of soda; 150 g (5 oz/1 cup) plain (all-purpose) flour; 1 tbsp whizzed stem ginger; 70 g (2$^1$/$_2$ oz/$^1$/$_2$ cup) brown sugar

**METHOD** Pre-heat the oven to 160°C/325°F/ Gas Mark 3. Line a baking sheet with baking parchment. Melt the butter together with the syrup in a saucepan and add the bicarbonate of soda – don't worry when it fizzes! Remove from the heat. Mix the flour, ginger and sugar together and then make a well in the middle. Pour in the syrup mixture and combine.

Taking a spoonful of mixture at a time, place on the baking sheet, making different shapes – rounds, semi-circles, and rectangles, for example. Bake for about 15 minutes, or until firm. Cool on a wire rack. Transfer the lemon cream fondue to a fondue pot and light the tealight to heat very gently. Hand-dip the ginger thins into the lemon cream fondue.

**STRAWBERRIES IN BALSAMIC VINEGAR** serves 6

**INGREDIENTS** 2 tbsp aged balsamic vinegar; 1 tbsp caster (superfine) sugar; 1 punnet (250–500 g/ 8 oz –1 lb) strawberries **METHOD** Mix the balsamic vinegar and sugar together in a big bowl and roll the strawberries in the mixture. Transfer the lemon cream fondue to a fondue pot and light the tealight to heat very gently. Skewer or hand-dip the strawberries into the lemon cream fondue.

# SIMPLE DIPPERS

There are all kinds of foods that you can dip into a fondue. Often, the best dippers of all are the simplest ones to prepare. Some dippers, like fruits and vegetables, are perfect for dipping in their natural state. Others that can be bought ready-made from a shop make equally simple, tasty dippers.

## BREAD

We have used just a few types of breads in our recipes, but these days there are many delicious breads available: organic, wheat-free, seeded, wholemeal, brown, white, olive, sun-dried tomato, ciabatta, focaccia – the list is endless. You can even buy a sweet bread or pastry, such as a brioche or a croissant, for dipping into a sweet fondue.

Tradition dictates that the bread used for cheese fondue should be a day or two old, and thus slightly stale. If the bread is too fresh, it will not hold the cheese, and will invariably break off and end up in the fondue! Another idea is to toast, grill, or even fry the bread in some olive oil until crisp. Breadsticks, cheese straws and crackers are also simple and delicious dipping options.

Bread is easiest to dip when cut into 2.5–4 cm (1–1$^1$/$_2$ in) cubes. If the pieces are bigger than that, it will be difficult to eat them. When cutting the bread, bear in mind that it's best if each cube retains some of the crust, as the crust will help keep the bread steady on the fork after it has been dipped into the fondue.

## CAKES, COOKIES AND BISCUITS

Cakes, cookies and biscuits come in all shapes, sizes and textures. Dense cakes and virtually any type of cookie or biscuit are perfect for dipping into all kinds of sweet fondues. As is the case with breads, cakes make better dippers when they are a day or two old, as they are less crumbly and thus less likely to fall off the fork. Try cutting cubes of day-old lemon or Madeira (pound) cake and skewering them for dipping. Some crunchier options include biscotti, ginger cookies, chocolate chip cookies – some people even like pretzels dipped into a chocolate fondue for that wonderful savoury-sweet taste sensation. For a rich taste, try spreading peanut butter on a cookie and dipping into some chocolate fondue. Delicious!

## VEGETABLES

Almost any vegetable can be dipped into a fondue. Make sure that your vegetables are fresh, especially if you are hand-dipping them (fresher vegetables are generally stiffer and thus easier to dip), and clean them thoroughly. Be sure to cut your vegetables into appropriate shapes for dipping. For example, sweet peppers are best cut into thicker strips, as thinner strips will be too flimsy and difficult to handle. Some vegetables, such as broccoli, cauliflower and asparagus, make very good dippers by virtue of having a stalk. These vegetables should be cut with some of the stalk still attached, and the floret should be placed into the fondue first. Florets are especially good for catching cheese fondue.

If you plan on dipping vegetables into a stock fondue, choose vegetables that cook fairly quickly, or your guests will be left waiting for their vegetables to cook! Mangetout (snow peas) and button mushrooms are particularly good vegetables for dipping into stock fondue, as they cook quickly and don't have to be cut. If you are using cylinder-shaped vegetables, such as carrots or courgettes (zucchini), try cutting them in a more interesting way than just a plain round shape. For example, you could cut straight down the middle lengthwise, then cut every 1 cm ($^3/_8$ in) on an angle, giving a stretched coin shape.

## FRUITS

Fondues are a great way to get the whole family eating lots of fresh ingredients, especially children who find dipping their own selection of food into fondue a lot more fun and interesting than the usual meal time experience. Every one of the sweet fondue recipes in this book can be dipped into with fresh fruits; the decision of which fruits to serve depends on which ones you fancy. Some common favourites include apples, bananas, strawberries and grapes, but don't forget about exotic fruits such as pineapples, figs, kiwis and lychees, to name a few – especially if you are having a fondue party with a relevant theme! Dried fruits also make delicious dippers, and they taste especially lovely when dipped in a red wine-based fondue (see our Mulled Wine Fondue recipe, page 62). Underripe fruits, such a pears, can be poached in sugar syrup, fruit juice or a fruity alcohol. Some fruits, such as apples, pears and grapes, can even be dipped in both sweet and savoury fondues.

While almost any fruit can be dipped into a fondue, very soft fruits, such as raspberries, blackcurrants and blueberries, are probably not right for fondue, as they are too small. You can, however, still serve them to your guests on the side, with the fondue dribbled onto them, like a sauce.

Small, firm fruits such as strawberries, kumquats, figs and cherries can be served as they are, and can be skewered or hand-dipped – as you like. They just need washing, rinsing and drying and they are ready to go.

If you are using large, round fruits, such as mangos, nectarines or peaches, you will need to cut them into slices. To do this, cut the fruit in half and remove the stone from the middle. Then cut each half into strips lengthwise. Don't cut the fruit strips too thin, however, or they will be too flimsy to hold the fondue and may even fall off your skewer. Aim for slices that are about 1 cm ($^3/_8$ in) wide.

Some fruits, such as apples, pears and oranges, need their pips removed before being cut into lengthwise strips. Other fruits, such as apples, pears, bananas and avocados, need to have lemon juice squeezed onto them to stop them from going brown. Depending on your taste, you may choose to peel the skin from your fruits, or you may want to keep them intact. We generally like to keep the skin on our fruit when we are serving it for fondue dipping – with the exception, of course, of fruit with inedible skin such as melon pieces or oranges!

# DIPPING TIPS

■ If your cheese fondue is too thin, thicken it by stirring in some more cheese. Another option is to dissolve one tablespoon of cornstarch into one tablespoon of the cooking liquid, then gradually stir the mixture into the simmering fondue until it reaches the right consistency.

■ If the fondue is too thick, just add more of the cooking liquid, warmed first in a small saucepan or a microwave oven. If it is lumpy or gritty, briskly whisk in one tablespoon of fresh lemon juice or vinegar.

■ Tell guests to give cheese fondue a good "figure eight" swirl with their forks as they dip to discourage the fondue from separating. They should also periodically scrape the bottom of the pan with their bread to keep the cheese on the bottom from burning.

■ When adding wine to a cheese fondue recipe, if possible use a dry or semi-dry wine, such as a Swiss Fendant, Sauvignon Blanc or a Riesling. These wines will help the proteins in the cheese to melt more smoothly.

■ All fondue food should be served in one- or two-bite pieces to allow for easy skewering or hand-dipping.

Some food items are already the right size and shape: strawberries, large marshmallows, small cookies, medium shrimp and large scallops, for example, are perfect as they are. Cut breads and cakes into 2.5–4 cm (1–1$^1$/$_2$ in) cubes, and meats and fish into $^1$/$_2$- to 1-inch cubes.

■ When eating any type of fondue food, remember you are sharing a communal pot, so try not to touch your lips or tongue to a fork that will be headed back into the fondue pot.

■ When cooking meat in a fondue pot, skewer each piece onto your fondue fork so that the tines protrude slightly. This will prevent the meat from sticking to the bottom of the pot.

■ When cooking food in oil or stock fondue, give your guests two forks: one for cooking and the other for eating. The cooking fork will be much too hot to eat from.

■ If you plan on serving hot oil or stock fondue at a party, we highly recommend that the party be sit-down style. Fondue pots are fairly sturdy, but there is always the chance that mingling guests or curious children might upset an unattended pot.

■ Be sure to provide your guests with an abundance of napkins, and cover the table with a washable tablecloth. Fondue-style meals can be very messy!

# TRADITIONS AND FORFEITS

There are many traditions associated with eating fondue. In Switzerland, fondue is usually eaten between October and April, when the evenings are longer, and people working in the outdoors can enjoy a long, relaxing evening over a bubbling fondue pot. Historically, villagers in the Alpine regions used to make fondue in the winter to use up their old, hard cheese and stale bread when other food was scarce, adding wine to help the cheese melt and, of course, to drink with it. But of course fondue can be eaten at any time: inside on a cold winter's evening, or in the garden on a summer's night. But be warned: with fondue comes forfeits, which can make for quite an amusing evening! One tradition dictates that if a piece of bread falls off your fork while you are swirling it around in the melted cheese, there is a forfeit to pay. If this happens to a woman, her forfeit is to kiss all the gentlemen at the table! If it happens to a man, then he must give the hostess a bottle of wine or a large glass of kirsch. If the same person drops their bread in the fondue a second time, he or she must host the next fondue party.

When an entire pot of cheese fondue has been eaten, look at the bottom of the pot and you will notice that a lovely brown crust of cheese has formed. This is called the croûton. It is customary to flambé the croûton in kirsch right inside the fondue pot. The host will then scrape the flambéd croûton off the bottom of the pan and distribute it amongst the guests to share. Delicious! While not a Swiss tradition, we think it is nice to serve a fresh green salad after a cheese fondue to help clear the palate after all that rich melted cheese.

In Switzerland, the tradition is not to drink while the fondue is being eaten, although it is customary to have a glass of kirsch halfway through the meal. Cold drinks are never served at a fondue meal, as the mixture of cold liquid and warm, melted cheese in the stomach can cause digestion problems. Very dry white wines, such as Riesling or Hock, can be served, as can warm drinks, including warm, unsweetened tea or warm fruit juice. Kirsch, schnapps or Glühwein are other possible serving alternatives. While stock, oil and dessert fondues don't have as much tradition as the famous cheese fondue, the same drink alternatives can equally be served with these types of fondue. Wine goes down very nicely with most stock and oil fondues, and a cold glass of good champagne or a cold dessert wine is lovely when served with any kind of dessert fondue.

# SUPPLIERS

Many large department stores carry fondue sets in their cookery departments. We have found that the selection increases around the holidays, but you can typically find the basics at any time of year. The following is a small selection of shops that stock fondue equipment.

## UK

**DEBENHAMS**

1 Henrietta Place

London W1

Tel: 0844 561 6161

*Locations throughout Britain.*

**HABITAT**

196 Tottenham Court Road

London W1

Tel: 020 7631 3880

**HEALS**

196 Tottenham Court Road

London W1

Tel: 020 7636 1666

## AUSTRALIA

**HOMEART**

Highpoint City Shopping Centre

Shop 3165, 200 Rosamond Road

Maribyrnong, VIC 3032

www.homeart.com.au

**HOMEWARE DIRECT**

www.homewaredirect.com

## MY HOUSE

Shop 2001 Westfield

Corner of Spring and Newlands Street

Bondi Junction, NSW 2022

www.myhouse.com.au

## NEW ZEALAND

**MILLY'S MAIL ORDER**

Freephone 0800 200 123

www.millys.co.nz

**MILLY'S KITCHEN, AUCKLAND**

· 273 Ponsonby Road, Ponsonby

· Level 1, 155-165 The Strand, Parnell

**BODUM HOMESTORE**

Two Double Seven Centre

277 Broadway, Newmarket

Auckland

Tel: (09) 529 4080 / 969 2620

**LIVING AND GIVING**

0800LIVING (0800 548 464)

www.livingandgiving.co.nz

*Stores nationwide.*

# INDEX